Guide to
Rocks & Minerals
of the Northwest

Stan Leaming & Chris Leaming

INTRODUCTION

This guide is intended to show some of the much-prized rocks and minerals of the northwest. Some are valued for their beauty when cut and polished. Others are prized for the economic value of the metals they contain, such as copper in chalcopyrite, or of some physical property of the mineral itself, such as the fibrous nature of asbestos. Still other minerals are valued for their crystal form, or, simply as examples of the great diversity in the mineral kingdom.

Minerals are made up of one or more elements. Gold (Au) is a single-element mineral. Quartz is a two-element mineral, silicon dioxide (SiO_2). Rhodonite is a three-element mineral, manganese silicate ($MnSiO_3$). Some minerals contain many elements, for example, jade, known as calcium magnesium iron hydrous silicate [Ca $(MgFe)_5$ Si_8O_{22} $(OH)_2$].

Rocks in turn are a mass, or aggregate, of one or more minerals. For example, marble is a mass of one mineral, calcite or calcium carbonate ($CaCO_3$). Granite is composed of several minerals; feldspar and quartz are always present and, in addition, several other minerals such as hornblend and biotite exist.

Rocks are divided into three classes: igneous, sedimentary, and metamorphic.

I Igneous Rocks

Igneous rocks are those derived from molten matter and include both the intrusive rocks, such as granite which cooled within the earth to form coarse-grained rocks, and the extrusive or volcanic rocks which poured out on the surface of the earth as lava flows and cooled quickly to fine-grained rocks. Some igneous rocks are granite, gabbro and syenite, basalt and rhyolite.

Sedimentary rock heavily eroded. Francois Lake, B.C.

Igneous rock with a black basalt intrusion Horseshoe Bay, B.C.

II Sedimentary Rocks

Sedimentary rocks are those derived from deposits in a fluid environment on the earth's crust. This fluid environment is usually water, but it may be air, as with volcanic ash. Sedimentary rocks are laid down in layers or beds which are essentially flat. Some are formed from pre-existing rocks by the erosive action of water, wind, and heat or cold. These are the clastic, or broken rocks, and include common rocks such as sandstone, shale and conglomerate.

Some sedimentary rocks are formed as chemical precipitates like some gypsum, some limestone, rock salt, flint, jasper, chert and travertine, while others result from the compaction of the shells of marine organisms. Thus, most limestone is a compaction of countless calcium carbonate shells of marine organisms.

III Metamorphic Rocks

Both igneous and sedimentary rocks may be affected by heat and pressure produced in new geological environments and form the third class — metamorphic rocks. Minerals typical of metamorphic action include kyanite, garnet and epidote. Metamorphic rocks include marble, quartzite, schist and gneiss.

Rock
Collecting

Cabochons
cut from various rocks.

An interest in minerals and rocks can range from a casual apprecia-
tion of one's surroundings and its building blocks, through varying
degrees of collecting samples as a rock hound, to making a profession
of studying geological formations as a geologist. Collecting can also be
broken down into categories depending upon the size of the samples.
Large boulders weighing several pounds are usually called museum or
field samples; fist-sized ones are called cabinet specimens; next are
thumbnail specimens and finally, come the tiny micro-mounts which
require a ten to thirty-power microscope for examination.

SOME FAVORITE LAPIDARY MINERALS

Jade

Jade is the name given to two different minerals. Strictly speaking they are mineral aggregates and are both composed of rather uncommon types of very common minerals.

The type of jade found in the northwest is called nephrite. It belongs to the amphibole group of minerals and is in fact iron-bearing tremolite. The formula is written $Ca_2 (MgFe)_5 Si_8O_{22} (OH)_2$. It is a calcium, magnesium, iron, hydrous silicate. Tremolite itself is not a rare mineral; it usually crystallizes in long fibres or prismatic crystals with good cleavage. In nephrite the crystals are microscopic-sized fibres bundled and felted together in a characteristic texture. This gives the rock great toughness.

Nephrite jade outcropping in the Cassiar Mountains.

Jade prospectors. Northern B.C.

Jade slab.
The white streak
is diopside.

A Jade boulder.
Northern B.C.

This boulder was named Bhudda's foot.
National Museum of Canada, Ottawa, Coll.

Jade made good tools and weapons for ancient man and when superseded by iron and steel, the material became more important as an art medium. Ancient peoples in China, New Zealand and Central America carved jade into a great many forms for ritual or decorative purposes. Modern lapidarists make use of jade for gemstones, book-ends, clockfaces, and so forth.

Jadeite is a member of the pyroxene group of minerals. Its formula is $Na\,Al\,Si_2\,O_6$ and it is a sodium aluminum silicate. Jadeite is reported from Washington but unconfirmed in British Columbia.

Jade (nephrite) is found from Alaska to California and is associated with serpentine rocks. All serpentine rocks should be regarded as potential sources of jade and prospected carefully. It is also found in Wyoming, but in a different geological setting.

While British Columbia has been a leader in the production of nephrite jade, large quantities are known in Alaska. Occurrences in Washington and Oregon seem to be smaller but it must not be assumed that further, larger discoveries will not be made.

For many years in the northwest, jade was found only as boulders, but by tracing these boulders to their source, prospectors discovered many in-situ deposits in British Columbia and the Yukon Territory.

Production from jade boulders, talus blocks and outcrops is simply a matter of cutting the rock into suitable sizes for handling. This also provides a means of judging the quality, for the weathered outer surface masks the true appearance; in fact, many boulders are not easily recognized as jade.

Fine nephrite carving by Alex Schick

Jade cabochon tie clasp

Jade clock

Jade pen holder with Taiwan carved figurines. B.C. Jade.

Vesuvianite

Vesuvianite.
Skihist Mountain, B.C.

Vesuvianite, also called idocrase or California Jade, while not true jade, may be an attractive lapidary material. It bears some resemblance to jadeite and has been mistaken for the more valuable "Oriental" or "Chinese" jade.

Vesuvianite is found on bars along the Fraser River in British Columbia, and in Oregon at the mouth of the Chetco River.

Rhodonite

Rhodonite from Mt. Higgins, WA., showing much dendritic material and color variations.

This pink silicate mineral occurs in small masses within sedimentary rocks. Commonly, it is partially altered to black manganese oxides giving it a variegated or streaked appearance. As a lapidary medium it was greatly prized in Tzarist Russia.

Rhodonite is fairly common in British Columbia where the material from Salt Spring Island is widely known. It occurs in Washington, Oregon, Montana and Alaska.

Rhodonite. Salt Spring Island, B.C.
Vancouver Island, B.C.

VOLCANIC ROCKS

These are the rocks which form by the cooling of lava, the hot liquid that extrudes from the depths of the earth through volcanic cones, or long fissures or cracks in the earth's crust.

At times, the eruption and cooling may be so rapid that the liquid becomes solid without any crystallization, forming a volcanic glass such as obsidian.

Volcanic rocks that cool more slowly commonly exhibit a columnar jointing such as the flow near Garibaldi, B.C.

When cooled under water, lava may form ellipsoidal-shaped outlines called pillows.

Some volcanic rocks have largely or partially cooled and crystallized within the earth before being spewed out on the surface where quick

Mahogany obsidian. Or. U.B.C. Coll. 20523.

Obsidian from Mount Edziza, B.C.

Columnar basalt, Green Lake, B.C.

cooling essentially chills the remaining liquid. This process produces the porphyries — rocks in which large crystals occur in a fine-grained matrix. Porphyries are sometimes called flower stones for those varieties in which crystals cluster together in simulated petal-like groups. In cooling, the gasses expand to form vesicles. If these round, almond-shaped vesicles are later filled with another mineral, such as agate, zeolite or epidote, they are called amygdules. The example below is both amygdaloidal and porphyritic.

Partially-filled crystal-lined cavieties are called vugs and also are common in volcanic rocks. The crystals may be quartz, calcite, zeolites, etc.

Amygdaloidal Porphyritic Lava. Copper River near Terrace, B.C. Contains pink feldspar crystals and green epidote filled vesicles.

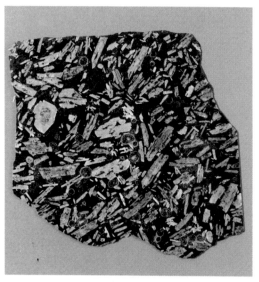

Bola tie clasp of porphyry.

"Mouse-track" porphyry. Vancouver Island, B.C.

Amygdaloidal basalt with agate and zeolites. Burns Lake, B.C.

Amygdaloidal basalt with zeolites and quartz crystal. Shaw Springs, B.C.

Pillow breccia "Dallasite". Fragments of volcanic rock cemented by quartz. Vancouver Island, B.C.

Calcite crystal in vug lined by quartz. Kamloops Lake, B.C.

Stellerite. Grant Co., Or. U.B.C. Coll. 22762

Mesolite needle crystal. Skookumchuck Dam, WA.

Chabazite, Yellow Lake, B.C.

Thomsonite.
Provencher Lake, B.C.

Stilbite. A zeolite mineral common in
Washington and British Columbia.

Zeolites are hydrous silicate minerals of calcium and/or sodium combined with aluminum. Some thirty species are known and volcanic rocks are the main host for many of them. Since the zeolites often line the vessels in crystalline form, they are much favored by micromounters.

Zeolites are common in the younger volcanic rocks of the northwest.

Ferrierite. North shore Kamloops Lake,
B.C. This zeolite is also found in WA.,

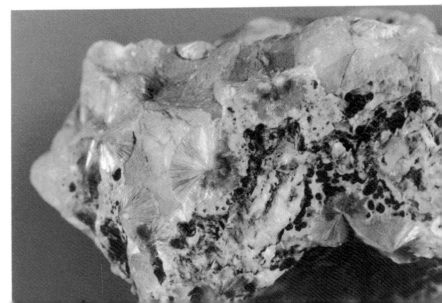

SILICA MINERALS

Silica minerals include quartz, chalcedony or agate, opal and jasper.They are all silica (SiO_2) chemically, and except for quartz, they are dense, micro-crystalline masses which means the individual crystals are too small to be recognizable. Quartz may also form macro crystals in suitable environments. In its large crystal form, quartz is readily distinguished from its relatives. However, differentiating opal from agate or a crystallized mass of quartz, may be more difficult.

Silica minerals are associated with many rocks. Agates are particularly abundant in volcanic rocks; jasper forms extensive sedimentary beds; opal replaces wood in many sedimentary rocks; and quartz crystals occur in igneous rocks particularly those called breccias.

Quartz

Quartz crystal. Harrison Lake, B.C.

Quartz is a very common mineral since it is the main constituent in sandstones and quartzites, and an essential part of the granitic rocks which make up a large proportion of the intrusive igneous rocks. Quartz commonly occurs as white to smoky hexagonal crystals -sometimes to more than a foot in length.

Quartz geode. St. Francisville, MT.
U.B.C. Coll. 20455

Geode — crystal quartz lined cavity in volcanic rock. WA.

Chalcedony and Agate

Chalcedony is very fine-grained crystalline quartz with a fibrous structure. Minor impurities give it color variations. Some of the variations in color and structure give rise to differing names. Thus, red or reddish-brown chalcedony is called carnelian. Chalcedony is an agate without variegation — it is not banded or patterned. Agate is a banded or variegated chalcedony. The color of agate can range from clear to reds, yellows, browns, greens and blues.

Agates are abundant in some varieties of volcanic rocks and may occur either as seams along fractures or in the openings left by escaping gas bubbles.

Chalcedony nodules. Jack Pot Rd., ID — Molsee Coll.

Brecciated or broken agate. WA.

Banded agate. Francois Lake, B.C.

Brecciated agate. Williams Lake, B.C.

Plume agate. OR.

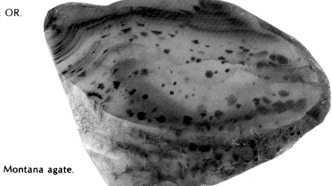

Montana agate.

Dendritic moss agate. Mt.

Green opal, Mount Savona, B.C.

Pink and white banded opal, Kamloops
Lake, B.C.

Opal

Opal is hydrous silica. The amount of water is variable and may be
as much as twenty percent or more, but it is commonly in the order
of five to ten percent. The water is not an essential ingredient of the
mineral. Although part of it seems to be trapped in the crystal
structure, most of the water appears to be held by adsorption and is
easily eliminated by heating or even exposure to a dry atmosphere.

Opal may be white to colorless and transparent, but impurities
give a wide range of colors and opacity. Precious opal is a rare
variety which, through optical effects, gives a rich play of colors.
Hyalite is the name given to clear, colorless opal. Opal is softer and
lighter than quartz which it resembles to some extent.

Opal is often the replacing medium in petrified wood and as
such it is fairly common material.

Opal is also formed inorganically by deposition or precipitation
from silica solutions, in openings in volcanic or sedimentary rocks.

Hungary has been famous for precious opal but is now eclipsed
by production from Australia. Mexico is also famous for opals.
Precious opal localities in the northwest are minor compared to
those of Australia and Mexico, but in Idaho, Washington and
Oregon, common opal is fairly widespread. South-central Washington
is famous for the huge logs of opalized wood that were once part of
a huge forest. The Horse Heaven Hills have been prolific for opals.

Specimens of precious opal have been reported from British
Columbia but no localities have yielded more than a few samples.
Common opal is not as abundant as agate.

Thundereggs

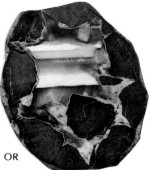

Thunderegg, Priday Ranch, OR

Thundereggs are nodules of agate or chalcedony which form in volcanic ash beds by a process of shrinkage.

They differ from geodes in that the thunderegg cavity is irregular rather than spheroidal and is usually filled.

In ideal thundereggs, the filling should display a five-pointed star. This is rarely displayed in perfection, but the examples shown here clearly illustrate that they are not like the gas-cavity filling of ordinary volcanic rocks geodes.

Oregon is the most prolific state for thundereggs and the Priday Ranch near Willowdale is one of the principal collecting sites.

Traditional five pointed star thunderegg.

Thunderegg, Priday Ranch, OR

A double thunderegg from Empire
Valley, B.C. Hillsdon Coll.

In this specimen the silica has mainly
crystallized as quartz.

Petrified Wood

Opalized Wood. Lincoln Co., Idaho.
U.B.C. Coll. 20642.

This fine lapidary material is formed by the replacement of the cell structure of the wood by silica — sometimes in the form of agate or opal. Oregon, Idaho and Washington have many fine occurrences of petrified wood. The colors can range from black to white, but browns, reds and yellows are the most common.

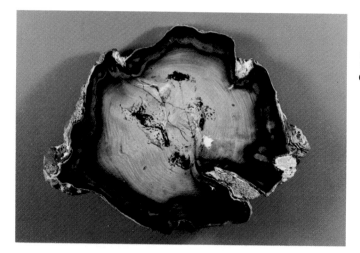

Agatized spruce wood. WA. Molsee Collection.

Opalized Wood. Craigmont Mine, Merritt, B.C.

Opalized Wood. Midway, B.C.

Petrified cypress. WA.

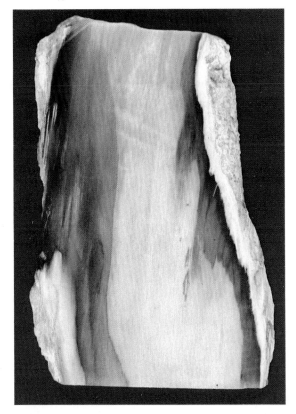

Jasper

Jasper. WA.

Jasper, Bruno Canyon, Idaho.

This dense, hard material is mainly silica, rendered opaque by impurities. Jasper is commonly red or reddish brown or yellow brown but may also be green. Hematite is responsible for the red varieties such as those pictured below.

Fort St. James, B.C.

Jasper breccia. Vancouver Island, B.C.

Copper Canyon, Vancouver Island, B.C.

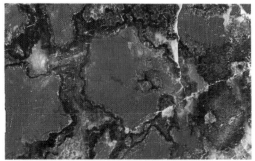

Picture Rocks

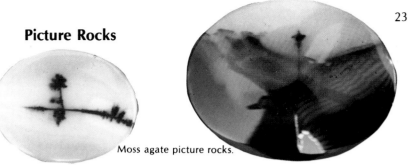

Moss agate picture rocks.

We include here a variety of rocks which when cut with a diamond saw reveal interesting patterns; sometimes they simulate natural scenes.

Red Shale baked by volcanic injections (black). Telkwa, B.C.

"Ocean-picture-rock" — an altered serpentine and quartz configuration. Midway, B.C.

CRYSTALS

Crystals are nature's naturally faceted gemstones. They are the regular polyhedral shapes bounded by plane faces and formed when a chemical substances changes, (under suitable conditions), from the state of a gas or liquid to a solid. Crystals are classified into six systems based on the symmetry of the faces in relation to three (or four) reference lines called crystallographic axes.

Isometric System

There is a large number of distinctive crystal forms in the isometric system. We illustrate here only four.

Octahedron: Fluorite. Birch Island, B.C.

Pyritohedron: the common form of the mineral pyrite B.C.

Cube, Galena.
Bluebell Mine, Riondel, B.C.

Dodecahedron: almandine garnets. Emerald Creek, ID.

Hexagonal System

Quartz crystal. Hope, B.C.

Hexagonal crystals have three or six sides.
The system includes such common minerals as quartz,
calcite and corundum. The most interesting forms of corundum are
rubies and sapphires.

Tourmaline showing three terminal
faces about the vertical axis. Black
tourmaline is common. B.C.

Apatite crystal. B.C.

Calcite — dog-tooth spar. MT.
Molsee Coll.

Tetragonal System

Zircon, apophyllite, vesuvianite and cassiterite are common representatives of this system.

Apophyllite.

Orthorhombic System

Aragonite.
Kluane Park, Yukon.

Barite
Rock Candy Mine,
north of
Greenwood, B.C.

Monoclinic System

Gypsum, epidote, orthoclase and realgar are all typical examples of monoclinic crystals.

Gypsum crystals. Drumheller, Alta. Good gypsum crystals are also found in B.C. and OR.

Lazulite crystals with wardite — phosphate minerals from northern Yukon Territory.

Realgar Crystals. Reward
Molsee Coll.

Triclinic System

Axinite and the plagioclase feldspar are typical triclinic crystals.

Plagioclase. Idaho.

Axinite. Skagit Bluffs, Hope-Princeton Highway, B.C.

ECONOMIC MINERALS

These minerals have monetary value for the contained metal or for some physical property of the mineral itself. The former group are called metallic ore minerals, the latter, non-metallic or industrial minerals.

Metallic Minerals

Magnetite crystal, Blue River, B.C.

Cobalt-Nickel Ore Minerals

Erythrite — pink cobalt bloom. Lemhi Co., ID. U.B.C. Coll. 3936.

Copper Ore Minerals

Covellite — contains 66% copper — hexagonal. Butte, MT.

Chalcopyrite — copper ore with malachite. Highland Valley, B.C.

Azurite from OK Mine, Milford, UT.

Silver Ore Minerals

Native silver with chalcite. Dankoe Mines, Keremeos, B.C.

Lead and Zinc Ore Minerals

Galena (blue-grey) lead ore and sphalerite (resinous brown) zinc ore. These two commonly occur together. Houston, B.C.

Lead and zinc commonly occur together as sulphide minerals galena and sphalerite. Galena may be silver-bearing. These are the most important lead and zinc minerals but others are found such as the zinc carbonate minerals.

Linarite — lead, copper ore — Marysville Dist., MT. U.B.C. Coll. 3009.

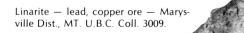

Smithsonite — zinc ore. Stanley, MT. U.B.C. Coll. 5873.

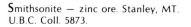

Non Metallic Minerals

Asbestos

Asbestos fibres are delicately fibrous and flexible so they can be woven. Asbestos is a form of serpentine.

Asbestos. Cassiar, B.C.

Kyanite

Kyanite is a useful refractory or heat resistance material and is used for the porcelain in spark plugs and furnace linings. It is a common metamorphic mineral. It occurs in British Columbia along the Columbia River north of Revelstoke.

Kyanite.
Lemhi Co., ID.
U.B.C. Coll
20439.

Vermiculite

This material includes several micaceous minerals, all with the property of expanding on heating. In some varieties, long worm-like threads are produced; hence the name vermicular, from the Latin for worms.

Vermiculite — Heat expanded on left. Lincoln Co., MT. U.B.C. Coll. 21232.

Magnesite

Magnesite — magnesium carbonate alteration in serpentine. Yalakom River, B.C.

Travertine. Lillooet, B.C.

Magnesite, or magnesium carbonate, is commonly associated with serpentine rocks from which it forms by the additon of carbon dioxide. A very large deposit of magnesite occurs in Washington near Chewelah where the mineral replaces limestone.

When used as a source of magnesium metal, magnesite is an ore mineral. When used for refractory bricks or for lapidary purposes, it is an industrial mineral.

Travertine

Travertine is banded calcium carbonate deposited from mineral springs. It is too soft for jewelry but is used as decorative rock. Much Mexican travertine (onyx) is carved into bookends and figurines.

Travertine. Kutcho Creek, Northern B.C.

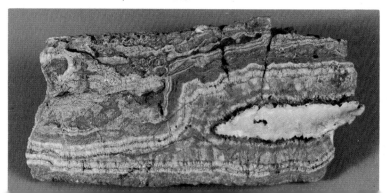